Dionis Castro Cabeza

Data Mining

Dionis Castro Cabeza

Data Mining

Introduction to Data Mining

ScienciaScripts

Imprint
Any brand names and product names mentioned in this book are subject to trademark, brand or patent protection and are trademarks or registered trademarks of their respective holders. The use of brand names, product names, common names, trade names, product descriptions etc. even without a particular marking in this work is in no way to be construed to mean that such names may be regarded as unrestricted in respect of trademark and brand protection legislation and could thus be used by anyone.

Cover image: www.ingimage.com

This book is a translation from the original published under ISBN 978-613-9-05898-3.

Publisher:
Sciencia Scripts
is a trademark of
Dodo Books Indian Ocean Ltd. and OmniScriptum S.R.L publishing group

120 High Road, East Finchley, London, N2 9ED, United Kingdom
Str. Armeneasca 28/1, office 1, Chisinau MD-2012, Republic of Moldova, Europe
Printed at: see last page
ISBN: 978-620-7-78581-0

Data Mining

Dionis Castro Cabeza

Content

Introduction

Data mining is a computer-aided technique used in analytics to process and explore large data sets.

It is a discipline that combines techniques from Artificial Intelligence, Computational Learning, Probability, Statistics, and Databases to extract useful information and knowledge from large amounts of data.

Its objective is to detect consistent patterns of behavior, or relationships between different fields in a database in order to apply them to new data sets.

Data mining can be defined as an analytical process, designed to explore large amounts of data, with the objective of finding relationships between different variables, in order to apply them to new data sets.

There are several definitions for the concept of Data Mining, but the essence of it is based on the concept of digging through stored information to discover useful elements from large amounts of stored data.

Data mining can be applied to different areas, such as marketing, healthcare, industry, among others. In marketing, for example, it can be used to segment markets, predict trends, or personalize offers.

In healthcare, it can be used to predict disease, improve medical care, or develop new treatments.

In industry, it can be used to improve product quality, optimize processes, or predict failures.

Data mining can be performed using different algorithms, such as Neural Networks, Decision Trees, Rule Induction, K-Nearest Neighbor, Logistic Regression, among others.

These algorithms can be applied to different types of data, such as numerical data, categorical data, or mixed data.

Data mining can be used in the process of knowledge discovery in databases. This process consists of several phases, such as data selection, data preparation, model selection, model evaluation, and visualization of the results.

Each phase requires different techniques, tools, and skills.

Data mining is related to other disciplines, such as statistics, artificial intelligence, data science, and computer science.

These disciplines provide the theoretical foundations, mathematical methods, and computer technologies necessary for data mining.

Data mining has several benefits, such as increased efficiency, increased effectiveness, increased competitiveness, and increased innovation.

Data mining also has several challenges, such as managing the quality of the data, managing the quantity of the data, managing the complexity of the algorithms, and managing the uncertainty of the results.

Data mining is a useful tool for knowledge and decision making in business.

Data mining can help businesses navigate familiar and unfamiliar waters, keep the barge afloat, and turn it into a vessel capable of sailing successfully.

Data mining is a technique that requires continuous training, constant updating, and constant adaptation.

Data mining is a technique that demands a commitment to learning, to progress, and to the future.

1.1.   Definition of Data Mining

Data mining, also known as data mining, is the process of analyzing large amounts of data to find trends and patterns. It is a technique used in data analysis to process and explore large data sets.

The objective is to detect information that is useful and can be applied to new data sets.

This technique is used in various fields, such as marketing, health and industry, to improve product quality, optimize processes and predict failures, among others.

Data mining is performed through different algorithms, such as neural networks, decision trees, rule induction, k-nearest neighbor, logistic regression, among others.

These algorithms can be applied to different types of data, such as numerical, categorical or mixed data.

Data mining is a process that requires continuous training, continuous updating and constant adaptation.

It is a tool that can help companies navigate familiar and unfamiliar waters, keep the ship afloat and turn it into a vessel capable of sailing successfully.

1.2.   Importance of Data Mining

Data mining is the process of analyzing large amounts of data to find trends and patterns. It is a technique used in data analysis to process and explore large data sets.

The objective is to detect information that is useful and can be applied to new data sets.

This technique is used in various fields, such as marketing, health and industry, to improve product quality, optimize processes and predict failures, among others.

Data mining is performed through different algorithms, such as neural networks, decision trees, rule induction, k-nearest neighbor, logistic regression, among others.

These algorithms can be applied to different types of data, such as numerical, categorical or mixed data.

Data mining is a process that requires continuous training, continuous updating and constant adaptation.

It is a tool that can help companies navigate both familiar and unfamiliar waters, keep the ship afloat and turn it into a vessel capable of sailing successfully.Data mining is important to companies for several reasons. First, it allows companies to analyze large amounts of data to find patterns and relationships that would otherwise be difficult to detect.

This can help companies make more informed decisions and improve their performance.

Second, data mining can help companies predict future trends and behaviors, allowing them to anticipate changes in the market and adapt in time.

Third, data mining can help companies personalize their products and services, which can increase customer satisfaction and improve loyalty.

Finally, data mining can help companies identify new business opportunities and develop new strategies.

Importance of Data Mining

Data mining is also important for companies because it allows them to get the most out of their data.

Companies generate and collect large amounts of data every day, but many of them do not know how to take advantage of all this potential.

Data mining can help companies transform their data into useful information and valuable insights.

This can help companies improve efficiency, reduce costs and increase revenues.

Data mining is also important for companies because it helps them compete in an increasingly competitive market.

Companies that use data mining can gain a competitive advantage over those that do not. Data mining allows companies to make faster and more accurate decisions, which can make the difference between success and failure.

In short, data mining is a data analysis technique that allows companies to analyze large amounts of data to find useful patterns and relationships.

Data mining is important for companies because it helps them make more informed decisions, predict future trends and behaviors, customize their products and services, identify new business opportunities and develop new strategies.

Data mining is also important for companies because it allows them to make the most of their data and helps them compete in an increasingly competitive marketplace.

1.3.   Data Mining Applications

Data mining is the process of analyzing large amounts of data to find trends and patterns. It is used in various fields, such as marketing, healthcare and industry, to improve product quality, optimize processes and predict failures, among others.

Data mining is performed through different algorithms, such as neural networks, decision trees, rule induction, k-nearest neighbor, logistic regression, among others.

These algorithms can be applied to different types of data, such as numerical, categorical or mixed data.

Data mining is a process that requires continuous training, continuous updating and constant adaptation.

It is a tool that can help companies navigate familiar and unfamiliar waters, keep the ship afloat and turn it into a vessel capable of sailing successfully.

There are several applications of data mining in different fields. In marketing, data mining is used to improve segmentation, predict customer behavior, develop customer profiles and identify cross-selling opportunities.

In healthcare, data mining is used to predict disease, improve medical care and develop new treatments.

In industry, data mining is used to improve product quality, optimize processes and predict failures.

In marketing, data mining is used to explore large databases and improve market segmentation. By analyzing the relationships between parameters such as age, gender and preferences, it is possible to guess customer behavior in order to target personalized loyalty or acquisition campaigns.

Data mining in marketing also predicts which users are likely to unsubscribe from a service, what interests them based on their searches, and what to include in marketing campaigns.

In the retail industry, data mining is used to identify product associations and decide how to place them in different areas of the store. It also detects which offers are most valued by customers and increases sales at checkout.

In the banking sector, data mining is used to better understand market risks. It is applied to credit rating and intelligent anti-fraud systems to analyze card movements, purchase patterns and customer financial data.

In short, data mining is the process of analyzing large amounts of data to find trends and patterns. It is used in various fields, such as marketing, healthcare and industry, to improve product quality, optimize processes and predict failures, among others.

Data mining is performed through different algorithms, such as neural networks, decision trees, rule induction, k-nearest neighbor, logistic regression, among others.

These algorithms can be applied to different types of data, such as numerical, categorical or mixed data.

Data mining is a process that requires continuous training, continuous updating and constant adaptation.

It is a tool that can help companies navigate familiar and unfamiliar waters, keep the ship afloat and turn it into a vessel capable of sailing successfully.

Data mining has several applications in different fields, such as marketing, healthcare and industry, where it is used to improve segmentation, predict customer behavior, develop customer profiles, identify cross-selling opportunities, predict diseases, improve medical care, develop new treatments, improve product quality, optimize processes and predict failures, among others.

Common use cases for data mining in business include:

Marketing: Data mining is used to explore large databases and improve market segmentation. It allows to analyze the relationships between parameters such as customer age, gender, tastes, etc., to predict their behavior and target personalized loyalty campaigns. It is also used to predict the propensity of users to unsubscribe from a service, identify interests based on searches, and optimize mailing lists to increase response rates.

Banking: In the banking sector, data mining is used to better understand market risks. It is applied to credit ratings and intelligent anti-fraud systems, analyzing purchase patterns, card movements, and customer financial data. It also enables banks to learn about customers' preferences and online habits to optimize sales management and comply with regulations.

Education: In education, data mining benefits educators by providing access to student data. This makes it possible to identify patterns of performance, personalize instruction, and improve the effectiveness of educational programs.

These are some of the most common use cases of data mining in business, covering areas such as marketing, banking, and education, where it is used to improve decision making, market segmentation, risk management, and personalization of educational services, among others.

2.   Data Mining Fundamentals

The fundamentals of data mining include extracting information from large amounts of data to discover patterns, profiles and trends by analyzing data using pattern recognition technologies.

Data mining is based on the interpretation of large amounts of data to find meaningful relationships or patterns.

This process involves identifying the data needed, selecting useful data, choosing the appropriate tools and techniques, and applying phases such as data selection, exploration and cleaning.

In addition, data mining makes it possible to explore information stored in databases for several years, using a client-server architecture and specialized tools to analyze and extract valuable knowledge.

2.1.   Basic Concepts

Data mining is a computer-aided technique used in analytics to process and explore large data sets.

It is a discipline that combines techniques from Artificial Intelligence, Computational Learning, Probability, Statistics, and Databases to extract useful information and knowledge from large amounts of data.

Its objective is to detect consistent patterns of behavior, or relationships between different fields in a database in order to apply them to new data sets.

Data mining can be defined as an analytical process, designed to explore large amounts of data, with the objective of finding relationships between different variables, in order to apply them to new data sets.

There are several definitions for the concept of Data Mining, but the essence of it is based on the concept of digging through stored information to discover useful elements from large amounts of stored data.

Data mining can be applied to different areas, such as marketing, health, industry, among others.

In marketing, for example, it can be used to segment markets, predict trends, or customize offers.

In healthcare, it can be used to predict disease, improve medical care, or develop new treatments.

In industry, it can be used to improve product quality, optimize processes, or predict failures.

Data mining can be performed using different algorithms, such as Neural Networks, Decision Trees, Rule Induction, K-Nearest Neighbor, Logistic Regression, among others.

These algorithms can be applied to different types of data, such as numerical data, categorical data, or mixed data.

Data mining is related to other disciplines, such as statistics, artificial intelligence, data science, and computer science.

These disciplines provide the theoretical foundations, mathematical methods, and computer technologies necessary for data mining.

Data mining has several benefits, such as increased efficiency, increased effectiveness, increased competitiveness, and increased innovation.

Data mining also has several challenges, such as managing the quality of the data, managing the quantity of the data, managing the complexity of the algorithms, and managing the uncertainty of the results.

Data mining is a useful tool for knowledge and decision making in business.

Data mining can help businesses navigate familiar and unfamiliar waters, keep the barge afloat, and turn it into a vessel capable of sailing successfully.

2.2. Data Mining Process

The data mining process involves several steps, including the creation, testing and use of data mining models. The process begins with defining the objectives and selecting the data to be analyzed. Once the data has been selected, it must be cleaned and prepared for analysis. This may involve removing or correcting errors, addressing missing or incomplete data, and transforming the data into a format that can be used by data mining algorithms.

The next step is to apply data mining techniques, which are based on algorithms. These techniques can identify patterns, correlations and other types of analysis in the data. Some common data mining techniques include association rules, artificial neural networks, and decision trees. These techniques can be used to identify patterns in the data, such as relationships between variables, and make predictions based on those patterns.

Once the data have been analyzed, the results must be evaluated to determine their usefulness and accuracy. This may involve comparing the results with known results or testing the results in real-world situations. The final step is to use the results to make informed decisions or take action based on the knowledge gained from the data mining process.

In summary, the data mining process involves several steps, including defining the objectives, selecting and preparing the data, applying data mining techniques, evaluating the results, and using the results to make informed decisions. By following this process, organizations can gain valuable insights from their data and use them to improve their operations, products and services.

The stages of the data mining process are as follows:

•   Definition of the objectives: In this stage, the objectives to be achieved with data mining are established, identifying what is to be discovered or predicted from the data.

•   Data selection and preparation: Relevant data are selected for analysis and prepared for processing, which involves cleaning them, correcting errors, dealing with missing data, and transforming them into a format suitable for analysis.

•   Application of data mining techniques: In this stage, data mining algorithms and techniques are applied to identify patterns, correlations and other forms of analysis in the data.

•   Evaluation of results: The results obtained are evaluated to determine their usefulness and accuracy, comparing them with known results or testing them in real-world situations.

•   Use of the results: Finally, the results obtained are used to make informed decisions or to act on the knowledge gained through the data mining process.

These steps are essential to successfully carry out a data mining process and obtain valuable information from large data sets.

2.3.   Techniques and Algorithms Used

Techniques and algorithms used in data mining include:

•   **Association techniques**: These techniques seek to identify relationships between variables in the data, such as the association rule that shows the probability of an event occurring given another event.

- **Classification Techniques**: These are used to categorize data into predefined classes, such as the decision tree algorithm that classifies data according to certain characteristics.
- **Clustering Techniques**: These techniques group similar data into clusters, such as the k-means algorithm that groups data into clusters based on their similarity.
- **Regression Techniques**: These are used to predict numerical values based on independent variables, such as linear regression that models the relationship between variables.
- **Outlier Detection**: These techniques identify unusual values in the data that may indicate errors or interesting patterns.
- **Sequential Patterns**: Used to discover temporal sequences in the data, as in time series analysis.

These techniques and algorithms are fundamental in the data mining process to discover patterns, relationships and valuable insights from large data sets.

The most commonly used data mining algorithms include:

Neural Networks: These algorithms mimic the functioning of the human brain to recognize complex patterns in data. They are particularly useful for tasks such as image and speech recognition. However, they can be computationally expensive and require a large amount of data to train.

Decision Trees: These algorithms use a hierarchical structure to classify data. They are easy to interpret and can handle both numerical and categorical data. However, they can be sensitive to small changes in the data and may not work well with large data sets.

Logistic Regression: This algorithm is used to predict a categorical variable based on one or more predictor variables. It is simple and fast, but may not work well with complex relationships between variables.

K-Nearest Neighbors: This algorithm classifies data based on similarity to nearest neighbors in a multidimensional space. It is simple and can handle both numerical and categorical data. However, it can be sensitive to the choice of the number of neighbors and may not work well with large data sets.

Support Vector Machines (SVM): These algorithms find the optimal hyperplane that separates classes in a multidimensional space. They are particularly useful for tasks such as text classification and image recognition. However, they can be computationally expensive and require a large amount of data to train.

Each of these algorithms has its own advantages and disadvantages, and the choice of algorithm will depend on the specific problem and data characteristics. It is important to consider factors such as the size and complexity of the data, the type of variables and the desired outcome when selecting an algorithm.

3. Data Preparation

Data preparation is a crucial step in the data mining process. It involves preparing and cleaning the data to ensure that it is in a format suitable for analysis. This step typically includes the following tasks:

Data cleaning: this involves identifying and correcting errors, inconsistencies and missing values in the data.

Data transformation: consists of converting the data to a format that is suitable for analysis. This may include normalizing the data, converting categorical data to numerical data, or aggregating data.

Data integration: this involves combining data from multiple sources into a single data set.

Data reduction: this involves reducing the size of the data set to make it more manageable for analysis. This may include the removal of redundant or irrelevant data, or the use of techniques such as dimensionality reduction.

Data discretization: this involves converting continuous data into discrete categories.

Data sampling: this involves selecting a subset of the data for analysis. This may be necessary when dealing with very large data sets.

Data partitioning: this involves dividing the data into training, validation and test sets.

Data preparation is an iterative and time-consuming process, but it is essential to ensure that the data are of high quality and suitable for analysis. It is important to carefully consider each of these tasks and ensure that the data are adequately prepared before moving to the next step in the data mining process.

To select the appropriate data mining technique for a specific project, the following steps can be followed:

Understand the problem: Clearly define the problem you are trying to solve and the objectives of the project.

Select the data mining technique: Depending on the problem and objectives, select the most appropriate data mining technique. For example, if the objective is to classify data, then decision trees or support vector machines may be appropriate. If the objective is to cluster data, then k-means or hierarchical clustering may be appropriate.

Prepare the data: Prepare the data for the selected data mining technique. This may include cleaning the data, transforming the data, and reducing the dimensionality of the data.

Apply the data mining technique: Apply the selected data mining technique to the prepared data.

Evaluate the results: Evaluate the results of the data mining technique to determine if it meets the project objectives.

Iterate : if the results are not satisfactory, iterate the process by selecting a different data mining technique or preparing the data in a different way.

It is important to note that the selection of the appropriate data mining technique depends on the problem and the objectives of the project, as well as the characteristics of the data. Therefore, it is important to have a thorough understanding of the problem and the data before selecting a data mining technique.

Regarding the sources provided, they offer information on the most advanced data mining algorithms used in the industry, the advantages and disadvantages of data mining, the analysis and application of data mining algorithms, and the use of data mining techniques in system monitoring.

These sources may be useful in understanding the different data mining techniques and their applications.

2.4.   Data Collection

Data collection is the process of gathering and measuring information on variables of interest in a systematically established manner that allows for answering research questions, testing hypotheses, and evaluating results.

In data mining, data collection is an essential step in the process, as it involves gathering and preparing data for analysis. This step includes identifying data sources, collecting and cleaning the data, and preprocessing the data to ensure its quality and suitability for analysis.

There are several methods for data collection, including:

• Surveys: Surveys are a common method of data collection and can be conducted online, over the phone or in person. Surveys can be used to collect data on a wide range of topics, from customer satisfaction to employee performance.

- Interviews: Interviews are another method of data collection and can be conducted in person, by telephone, or by videoconference. Interviews can be used to gather detailed information on a specific topic or to gain a deeper understanding of a particular topic.
- Observation: Observation involves observing and recording the behavior of individuals or groups in a natural setting. This method can be used to collect data on a wide range of topics, from consumer behavior to employee performance.
- Experiments: Experiments involve manipulating one or more variables and measuring the effect on a dependent variable. This method is often used in scientific research to test hypotheses and evaluate results.
- Secondary data: Secondary data is data that has already been collected by someone else. This may include data from government databases, industry reports or academic studies.

Data collection is a critical step in the data mining process and it is important to ensure that the data are of high quality and suitable for analysis. This can be achieved through careful planning, systematic data collection, and rigorous data cleaning and preprocessing.

As for the sources provided, they offer information on the most advanced data mining algorithms used in the industry, the advantages and disadvantages of data mining, the analysis and application of data mining algorithms, and the use of data mining techniques in system monitoring. These sources may be useful in understanding the different data mining techniques and their applications.

2.5. Data Cleansing

Data cleaning, also known as data cleansing or data cleaning, is the process of identifying and correcting or removing errors, inconsistencies and inaccuracies in a data set. The goal of data cleaning is to improve the quality of the data and make it more reliable and useful for analysis and decision making.

Data cleansing typically involves several steps, including:

- Data profiling: involves analyzing data to identify patterns, inconsistencies and possible errors.
- Data standardization: this involves converting data to a consistent format, such as standardizing date formats or converting abbreviations to their full forms.
- Data deduplication: involves identifying and eliminating duplicate records to avoid biases and inaccuracies in the analysis.
- Data validation: this involves comparing data with external sources or business rules to ensure accuracy.

- Data enrichment: this involves adding missing data or updating obsolete data to improve the completeness and accuracy of the dataset.

Data cleansing is an important step in the data preparation process, as it helps ensure that data is of high quality and can be used effectively for analysis and decision making. According to a study by Experian, poor data quality can cost companies an average of 12% of their revenue, highlighting the importance of data cleansing for businesses.

There are several tools and techniques available for data cleansing, including manual data cleansing, automated data cleansing and machine learning-based data cleansing. The choice of tool or technique will depend on the size and complexity of the data set, as well as the specific needs and objectives of the organization.

In summary, data cleaning is a critical step in the data preparation process that involves identifying and correcting errors and inconsistencies in a data set. By improving the quality of the data, data cleaning can help ensure that it is reliable and useful for analysis and decision making.

Data cleansing is a crucial process in data mining, as it allows improving data quality and obtaining reliable and valuable information for decision making.

Data cleansing consists of correcting incorrect, incomplete, duplicate or erroneous data, which improves the accuracy of analysis and decision making.

Data cleansing is a process prior to the ETL (extraction, transformation and loading) of data into a company's data management system.

Data cleansing is performed by data analysts or data engineers, who not only study the data, but also clean it.

Data cleaning is important because without quality data, the reports that are produced with them will not be completely reliable, let alone the decisions that are made about them.

Proper data cleansing or data cleaning helps the business to have a solid data base on which to start making decisions.

In addition, data cleansing helps to have more orderly business data, avoid data errors, improve productivity, reduce costs and increase sales.

Data cleansing is a necessary step prior to data mining, as it improves the accuracy of analysis and decision making.

Data cleansing is not only a necessary step before data mining, but also a valuable one, as it improves data quality and the accuracy of analyses

Data cleansing is a process prior to the extraction, transformation and loading of data into a company's data management system.

Data cleansing is performed by data analysts or data engineers, who not only study the data, but also clean it.

Data cleansing is important because without quality data, the reports produced from it will not be fully reliable, let alone the decisions made about it.

A correct data cleansing or data cleaning helps the business to have a solid data base on which to start making decisions.

In addition, data cleansing helps to have more orderly business data, avoid data errors, improve productivity, reduce costs and increase sales.

Data cleansing is a necessary step before data mining, as it improves the accuracy of analysis and decision making.

Data cleansing is not only a necessary step before data mining, but also a valuable one, as it improves data quality and analysis accuracy.

Data cleansing is a process prior to the extraction, transformation and loading of data into a company's data management system.

Data cleansing is performed by data analysts or data engineers, who not only study the data, but also clean it.

Data cleansing is important because without quality data, the reports produced from it will not be fully reliable, let alone the decisions made about it.

Proper data cleansing or data cleaning helps the business to have a solid data base on which to start making decisions.

In addition, data cleansing helps to have more orderly business data, avoid data errors, improve productivity, reduce costs and increase sales.

Data cleansing is a necessary step prior to data mining, as it improves the accuracy of analysis and decision making.

Data cleansing is not only a necessary step before data mining, but also a valuable one, as it improves data quality and analysis accuracy.

Data cleansing is a process prior to the extraction, transformation and loading of data into a company's data management system.

Data cleansing is performed by data analysts or data engineers, who not only study the data, but also clean it.

Data cleansing is important because without quality data, the reports produced from it will not be fully reliable, let alone the decisions made about it.

A correct data cleansing or data cleaning helps the business to have a solid data base on which to start making decisions.

In addition, data cleansing helps to have more orderly business data, avoid data errors, improve productivity, reduce costs and increase sales.

Data cleansing is a necessary step before data mining, as it improves the accuracy of analysis and decision making.

Data cleansing is not only a necessary step before data mining, but also a valuable one, as it improves data quality and analysis accuracy.

Data cleansing is a process prior to the extraction, transformation and loading of data into a company's data management system.

Data cleansing is performed by data analysts or data engineers, who not only study the data, but also clean it.

Data cleansing is important because without quality data, the reports produced from it will not be fully reliable, let alone the decisions made about it.

A correct data cleansing or data cleaning helps the business to have a solid data base on which to start making decisions.

In addition, data cleansing helps to have more orderly business data, avoid data errors, improve productivity, reduce costs and increase sales.

Data cleansing is a necessary step before data mining, as it improves the accuracy of analysis and decision making.

Data cleansing is not only a necessary step before data mining, but also a valuable one, as it improves data quality and analysis accuracy.

Data cleansing is a process prior to the extraction, transformation and loading of data into a company's data management system.

Data cleansing is performed by data analysts or data engineers, who not only study the data, but also clean it.

Data cleansing is important because without quality data, the reports produced from it will not be fully reliable, let alone the decisions made about it.

A correct data cleansing or data cleaning helps the business to have a solid data base on which to start making decisions.

In addition, data cleansing helps to have more orderly business data, avoid data errors, improve productivity, reduce costs and increase sales.

Data cleansing is a necessary step before data mining, as it improves the accuracy of analysis and decision making.

Data cleansing is not only a necessary step before data mining, but also a valuable one, as it improves data quality and analysis accuracy.

Data cleansing is a process prior to the extraction, transformation and loading of data into a company's data management system.

Data cleansing is performed by data analysts or data engineers, who not only study the data, but also clean it.

Data cleansing is important because without quality data, the reports produced from it will not be entirely reliable, let alone the decisions made about it.

A correct data cleansing or data cleaning helps the business to have a solid data base on which to start making decisions.

In addition, data cleansing helps to have more orderly business data, avoid data errors, improve productivity, reduce costs and increase sales.

Data cleansing is a necessary step before data mining, as it improves the accuracy of analysis and decision making.

Data cleansing is not only a necessary step before data mining, but also a valuable one, as it improves data quality and analysis accuracy.

2.6.   Data Transformation

Data transformation is the process of converting data from one format to another, or from one structure to another, to make it more suitable for analysis or processing. This process is often necessary in data mining, as raw data collected from various sources may not be in a format suitable for analysis.

There are several techniques used in data transformation, including:

Data normalization: this involves scaling the numerical data to a common range, usually between 0 and 1, to prevent differences in scales from affecting the analysis.

Data aggregation: this involves combining data from multiple sources or multiple records into a single record to reduce the complexity of the data and make it more manageable.

Data discretization: involves converting continuous data into discrete categories or ranges, so that they are easier to analyze and interpret.

Data coding: Involves converting categorical data into numerical data, so that they are easier to analyze and interpret.

Data cleaning: Involves removing or correcting errors, inconsistencies or missing values in the data to improve the quality of the data and make it more reliable.

The choice of data transformation techniques depends on the nature of the data and the objectives of the analysis. It is important to carefully consider the implications of each transformation technique, as they may affect the results of the analysis.

The benefits of data transformation in data mining include:

Improved data quality: data transformation can help improve data quality by eliminating errors, inconsistencies or missing values.

Simplified data: data transformation can help simplify data, reducing its complexity and making it more manageable.

Improved analysis: data transformation can help improve analysis, making data more suitable for analysis and processing.

Improved interpretation: data transformation can help improve the interpretation of results by making the data easier to understand and interpret.

In general, data transformation is an essential step in the data mining process, as it helps to prepare the data for analysis and processing, and can significantly improve the quality and reliability of the results.

2.7. Data Integration

Data integration is a fundamental process that enables companies to consume, combine and leverage all types of data, ensuring that it is cleansed and error-free to optimize its usefulness to the business.

This process is essential for organizations with diverse and distributed environments, as it allows them to unify siloed and disconnected data, providing a unified view of the business and facilitating decision making based on accurate information.

Data integration has evolved over time and has been a challenge since the early days of business systems in the 1980s.

Today, data integration has become more holistic, combining data and application integration disciplines in a comprehensive effort to support all types of integration in a hybrid environment.

In addition, data intelligence, gained through data integration, is crucial for organizations, as it enables them to consume, combine and deliver data to meet process and application requirements, driving strategic decisions based on intelligent data.

Data orchestration goes beyond integration, combining data discovery, preparation, integration, processing and connection across multiple complex environments.

In short, data integration is a strategic process that combines data from multiple sources to provide organizations with a unified view and facilitate decision making based on accurate and reliable information.

Best practices for data integration include:

• Planning and design: Proper planning and design are crucial to successful data integration. This includes identifying business objectives and data requirements, modeling data, and selecting sources and targets.
• Extraction, Transformation and Loading (ETL): ETL is a key component of data integration, which involves extracting data from sources, transforming it to a consistent format, and loading it into a target system.
• Data quality: Ensuring data quality is essential for successful data integration. This includes data cleansing, standardization and validation to ensure accurate and consistent data.
• Security and privacy: Ensuring data security and privacy is critical to successful data integration. This includes implementing appropriate access controls, encryption techniques and anonymization.
• Monitoring and maintenance: Regular monitoring and maintenance of data integration processes are essential to ensure continued success. This includes monitoring data quality, identifying and resolving errors, and updating data mapping and transformation rules as needed.

By following these best practices, organizations can ensure successful data integration and maximize the value of their data assets.

3. Exploratory Data Analysis

Exploratory Data Analysis (EDA) is a statistical technique used to analyze and summarize data sets. Its main objective is to identify patterns, trends and relationships within the data, as well as to detect anomalies or outliers.

DEA is used to explore the data before making assumptions and is a crucial step in the data analysis process.

There are different types of DEA, such as univariate, bivariate and multivariate analysis.

Univariate analysis focuses on a single variable, while bivariate analysis explores the relationship between two variables. Multivariate analysis, on the other hand, examines the relationship between more than two variables.

DEA is a critical step in the data analysis process, as it helps to identify patterns and relationships within the data that may not be immediately apparent. It is also used to detect anomalies or outliers, which can have a significant impact on the results of the analysis.

A series of steps, such as data cleansing, data visualization and data summarization, are required to perform an AED.

Data cleaning is the process of identifying and correcting errors or inconsistencies in the data, while data visualization involves the creation of graphs and tables to represent the data in a more visually appealing way.

Data summarization, on the other hand, involves calculating statistical measures, such as mean, median and standard deviation, to summarize the data.

In summary, AED is a statistical technique used to analyze and summarize data sets, with the main objective of identifying patterns, trends and relationships within the data, as well as detecting anomalies or outliers. It is a crucial step in the data analysis process, and a series of steps must be followed to perform it correctly.

The main techniques used in exploratory data analysis include:

- Data visualization: This technique involves the creation of graphs and visualizations to represent data visually, which facilitates the identification of patterns, trends, and relationships in the data
- Correlation analysis: Used to examine the relationship between two or more variables, which helps to understand how they vary together and whether there is any relationship between them.
- Identification of missing data: This technique consists of identifying and managing missing data in the dataset, as the presence of missing data can affect the quality of the analysis
- Outlier detection: This refers to identifying outliers in the data, which can distort the results of the analysis and lead to erroneous conclusions if not handled properly.

• Descriptive analysis: This technique focuses on summarizing and describing the main characteristics of the data set, extracting its most representative features to better understand the information it contains.

• These techniques are fundamental in exploratory data analysis, as they allow exploring, understanding and drawing initial conclusions about the data before applying more advanced statistical techniques.

3.1.   Descriptive Statistics

Descriptive statistics is the branch of statistics that deals with the collection, storage, arrangement, tabulation and calculation of parameters of a set of data.

It is used to describe, summarize and present the behavior of data, translating it into understandable information.

This approach is essential to represent data graphically through tables and figures, quantify them and make them understandable.

The main types of statistical measures used in descriptive statistics are:

Measures of central tendency: These measures indicate the central position or the most representative value of a data set. The most common measures of central tendency are the mean, median and mode.

Measures of dispersion: These measures indicate the degree of dispersion or variability of a data set. The most common measures of dispersion are range, variance and standard deviation.

Shape measures: These measures indicate the shape or distribution of a data set. The most common shape measures are skewness and kurtosis.

Descriptive statistics are used in various fields, such as business, economics, social sciences and natural sciences, to analyze and interpret data and make informed decisions.

It is an essential tool for data analysis and is used in various applications such as data visualization, data summarization and data description.

In summary, descriptive statistics is a branch of statistics that deals with the collection, storage, ordering, tabulation and calculation of parameters of a data set. It is used to describe, summarize and present the behavior of data, translating it into understandable information. The main types of statistical measures used in descriptive statistics are measures of central tendency, measures of dispersion and measures of shape.

Descriptive statistics are a crucial part of data mining, as they help to understand and summarize the main characteristics of a data set. They are used to describe the central tendency, dispersion and shape of the data, among other characteristics. In the context of data mining, statistical techniques are applied to large data sets to extract relevant information and patterns that can be used for decision making and predictive modeling.

Some of the most commonly used statistical measures in data mining include mean, median, mode, variance, standard deviation, skewness and kurtosis. These measures help to describe the distribution of the data and to identify outliers or anomalies that may require further investigation.

In addition to statistical measures, data mining also uses data visualization techniques to represent data in a more intuitive and understandable way. These techniques include histograms, box plots, scatter plots and heat maps, among others.

In general, statistical techniques and data visualization are essential tools in data mining, as they help to extract meaningful information from large and complex data sets.

3.2. Data Visualization

Data visualization is a fundamental technique in data analysis that consists of representing information graphically to facilitate understanding, identify patterns, trends and relationships, and effectively communicate findings. Data visualization is a powerful tool for transforming complex data into clear and meaningful graphics, which facilitates informed decision making.

Some of the most commonly used data visualization techniques include:

- Bar charts: used to compare categories or to show the distribution of categorical data.
- Line graphs: These are useful for showing trends over time or in ordered sequences.
- Scatter diagrams: They allow visualizing the relationship between two variables and detecting patterns or correlations.
- Histograms: They show the distribution of numerical data in intervals or classes.
- Pie charts: Used to represent the proportion of different categories in a data set.

In addition to these basic techniques, advanced data visualization tools, such as heat maps, box and whisker plots, bubble charts, and interactive visualizations, allow you to explore and analyze data in more depth and detail.

Data visualization is an essential part of the data analysis process, as it helps to identify patterns, trends and relationships that may not be evident in the raw data. By presenting information visually, data interpretation is facilitated and data-driven decision making is improved.

3.3.   Correlation Analysis

Evaluation analysis is a statistical technique used to determine the relationship between variables. It provides information on the relationship between variables, and the strength of the correlation is determined by the correlation coefficient, which varies from -1 to +1.

Correlation analysis can be used to make a statement about the strength and direction of the correlation.

Correlation and causation are related but not the same thing. If correlation analysis shows that two characteristics are related, it can be further tested whether one characteristic can be used to predict the other. However, correlations do not necessarily imply causal relationships. Therefore, correlations should be investigated in more detail and should never be interpreted immediately in terms of content, despite the apparent relationship.

The correlation coefficient can take values between -1 and +1. A positive correlation indicates that when the magnitude of one variable increases, the other variable also increases. A negative correlation indicates that when the magnitude of one variable increases, the other variable decreases.

The strength of the linear relationship increases as the correlation coefficient approaches -1 or +1.

The correlation coefficient is calculated using the covariance formula between two variables divided by the product of the standard deviation of each variable.

Covariance measures the degree of linear relationship between two variables and standard deviation measures the dispersion of a variable with respect to its mean value.

There are different methods for calculating the correlation coefficient, such as Pearson's correlation coefficient, Spearman's correlation coefficient and Kendall's correlation coefficient.

Pearson's correlation coefficient measures the linear relationship between two variables, while Spearman's and Kendall's correlation coefficients measure the monotonic relationship between two variables.

The correlation coefficient is a useful tool for predicting the behavior of one variable based on the behavior of another variable. However, it is essential to interpret the results correctly and to consider other factors that may influence the relationship between variables.

Correlation analysis is a fundamental technique in data mining that helps to identify the relationship between two variables. It is used to measure the strength and direction of the relationship between two or more variables. Correlation analysis is used in a variety of fields, including finance, marketing, health, and social sciences, among others.

The correlation coefficient is a statistical measure that indicates the strength and direction of the relationship between two variables. The correlation coefficient can take values between -1 and 1, where a value close to 1 indicates a strong positive correlation, a value close to -1 indicates a strong negative correlation and a value close to 0 indicates no correlation.

Correlation analysis is used to identify patterns and relationships in the data that may not be evident by other statistical measures. It is also used to identify outliers and anomalies in the data that may affect the analysis.

Correlation analysis is used in various data mining techniques, such as regression analysis, clustering and classification. Regression analysis is used to establish a relationship between variables and predict values based on that relationship. Clustering is used to group similar data points and classification is used to assign data points to predefined categories based on their characteristics.

Correlation analysis is also used in exploratory data analysis, where it helps to identify patterns and relationships in the data. It is used to summarize and describe the data, providing a better understanding of the data before applying more advanced data mining techniques.

In summary, correlation analysis is a fundamental technique in data mining that helps to identify the relationship between two variables. It is used to measure the strength and direction of the relationship between two or more variables and is used in various data mining techniques such as regression analysis, clustering and classification. It is also used in exploratory data analysis to summarize and describe the data, providing a better understanding of the data before applying more advanced data mining techniques.

4.   Data Modeling

Data modeling is the process of creating a mathematical model that represents the relationship between variables in a data set. The goal of data modeling is to identify patterns and relationships in the data that can be used to make predictions or draw conclusions.Data modeling involves several steps, including:

- Data preparation: this involves cleaning and transforming the data to make it suitable for analysis.
- Exploratory data analysis: this involves analyzing data to identify patterns and relationships.
- Model selection: involves choosing an appropriate mathematical model to represent the data.
- Model fitting: involves estimating the model parameters using the data.

- Model evaluation: this involves evaluating model performance using metrics such as accuracy, precision, recall and F1 score.

There are several types of data models, including:

- Regression models: these models are used to predict a continuous variable as a function of one or more independent variables.
- Classification models: these models are used to predict a categorical variable as a function of one or more independent variables.
- Clustering models: these models are used to group similar data points.
- Time series models: these models are used to predict future values of a variable based on past values.
- Neural network models: these models are used to model complex relationships between variables using artificial neural networks.

Data modeling is an important step in data mining, as it enables the creation of predictive models that can be used to make informed decisions. By identifying patterns and relationships in data, data models can provide insight into the underlying processes that generate the data.

In summary, data modeling is the process of creating a mathematical model that represents the relationship between variables in a data set. It involves several steps, including data preparation, exploratory data analysis, model selection, model fitting, and model evaluation. There are several types of data models, including regression models, classification models, clustering models, time series models, and neural network models. Data modeling is an important step in data mining, as it enables the creation of predictive models that can be used to make informed decisions.

Data modeling in data mining refers to the process of creating mathematical models based on data to identify patterns and relationships. These models can be used to make predictions or draw conclusions. Data modeling involves several steps, including data preparation, exploratory data analysis, model selection, model fitting, and model evaluation.

There are several types of data models used in data mining, including regression models, classification models, clustering models, time series models, and neural network models.

The choice of model depends on the type of data and the problem to be solved.

Data modeling is an important step in data mining, as it enables the creation of predictive models that can be used to make informed decisions. By identifying patterns and relationships in the data, data models can provide insight into the underlying processes that generate the data.

In summary, data modeling in data mining is the process of creating mathematical models based on data to identify patterns and relationships. These models can be used to make predictions or draw conclusions. Data modeling involves several steps, including data preparation, exploratory data analysis, model selection, model fitting, and model evaluation. There are several types of data models used in data mining, including regression models, classification models, clustering models, time series models, and neural network models. Data modeling is an important step in data mining, as it enables the creation of predictive models that can be used to make informed decisions.

4.1. Variable Selection

Variable selection is a process in which the most relevant and significant variables in a data set are identified and selected. This is done in order to improve the accuracy and efficiency of machine learning and data mining algorithms.

There are different methods and approaches for the selection of variables, some of them are:

•	**Filter methods**: They are based on the evaluation of each variable individually and select those that have a greater relevance or relationship with the target variable.
•	**Wrapper methods**: They are based on the evaluation of subsets of variables and select those that provide the best accuracy in the predictive model.
•	**Embedded methods**: They are integrated within the machine learning algorithm itself and select the most relevant variables during the training process.

Variable selection can be supervised or unsupervised, depending on whether or not the target variable is known.

In supervised variable selection, the target variable is used to assess the relevance of the variables, whereas in unsupervised variable selection, metrics such as entropy or inter-cluster distance are used to assess the relevance of the variables.

Variable selection is an important technique in data mining and machine learning, as it helps to reduce model complexity, improve accuracy and efficiency, and facilitate interpretation of results.

Variable selection can be performed using different algorithms and techniques, such as linear regression, logistic regression, decision trees, random forests, artificial neural networks, and genetic algorithms, among others.

Variable selection can also help identify and eliminate redundant or irrelevant variables, which can improve the performance and efficiency of machine learning and data mining algorithms.

In summary, variable selection is an important process in data mining and machine learning, which helps to identify and select the most relevant and significant variables from a dataset, improving the accuracy and efficiency of algorithms and facilitating the interpretation of results

Variable selection in data mining is a technique used to identify and select the most relevant and significant variables in a data set, in order to improve the accuracy and efficiency of machine learning and data mining algorithms.

Variable selection helps to solve two problems: having too much low-value data or too little high-value data.

There are different methods and approaches for variable selection, such as the Filter, Wrapper, and Embedded methods.

Variable selection can be supervised or unsupervised, depending on whether or not the target variable is known.

In supervised variable selection, the target variable is used to assess the relevance of the variables, whereas in unsupervised variable selection, metrics such as entropy or inter-cluster distance are used to assess the relevance of the variables.

Variable selection is an important technique in data mining and machine learning, as it helps to reduce the complexity of models, improve accuracy and efficiency, and facilitate interpretation of results

Variable selection can be performed using different algorithms and techniques, such as linear regression, logistic regression, decision trees, random forests, artificial neural networks, and genetic algorithms, among others.

Variable selection can also help identify and eliminate redundant or irrelevant variables, which can improve the performance and efficiency of machine learning and data mining algorithms.

In summary, variable selection is an important technique in data mining and machine learning, which helps to identify and select the most relevant and significant variables in a data set, improving the accuracy and efficiency of algorithms and facilitating the interpretation of results.

4.2.   Modeling Methods

Based on the resources provided, modeling methods in the context of data mining include techniques such as decision tree, neural network, statistical modeling, association rules, clustering, and genetic algorithms.

These methods are used to analyze large data sets and discover patterns, relationships, and hidden trends in the information.

- **Decision tree**: Tree structure that helps to represent problems and sequences in the data, where decision nodes and chance nodes play a crucial role.
- **Neural network**: Based on the functioning of human neurons, this technique uses input, output and hidden nodes to process information and learn patterns.
- **Statistical modeling**: Uses mathematical equations to predict outcomes based on relationships between variables in the data.
- **Association rules**: Finds combinations of items that occur most frequently in a database, as in the case of associating a customer's purchase intent with other products
- **Clustering**: Grouping elements in data sets with similarities, allowing the identification of patterns and relationships between the data
- **Genetic algorithms**: Based on the theory of evolution, these algorithms help to find optimal solutions to complex problems.

These modeling methods are fundamental in data mining, as they allow extracting relevant information, predicting outcomes, and discovering meaningful patterns in large data sets, which is crucial for informed decision making in business and other industries.

The most commonly used tools for data modeling in data mining include:

Orange: A tool that offers a seamless software for developing data mining processes, with widgets for visualization and processing. It is written in Python and is easy to use.

Rapid Miner: a platform that focuses on analytics and business intelligence, with a fast data delivery process and easy-to-use frameworks for data mining.

Teradata: a database that collects specific information on sales, customer preferences and product placement, ideal for sales-focused data mining.

KNIME: an open source tool that integrates data import, preparation, exploration and modeling, with an easy-to-use interface and hundreds of nodes for different actions.

Xplenty: a no-code software that helps companies create data pipelines easily, integrating all data sources and creating predictive models.

Rapid Miner Studio Free: a free open source tool based on a Java engine, with applications for text mining, machine learning and predictive analytics.

WEKA : a machine learning software that includes tools for data preprocessing, classification, clustering and association rules.

These tools offer different functionalities and are used for different purposes, but all are useful for data modeling in data mining.

4.3.   Model Evaluation

Model evaluation in data mining is a crucial step that helps to assess the performance and accuracy of the generated models. The evaluation process involves the use of various tools and techniques to test the models with a data set and compare their results with the actual results.

One of the most widely used tools for data mining is KNIME, which integrates the main functionalities for data mining projects, including data import, preparation, exploration, model building, validation and reporting. KNIME offers hundreds of nodes that provide different types of actions, such as data integration and manipulation, visualization, model building, validation, report generation and data writing. It also supports integrations with Java, Python, R and WEKA, providing the flexibility to program custom functions within a workflow.

Another important aspect of model evaluation is feature selection, which helps to solve the problem of having too much irrelevant data or too little valuable data. Feature selection involves reducing the inputs for processing and analysis or finding the most meaningful inputs. It is fundamental to creating a proper model, as it reduces cardinality and improves the quality of the model. It also makes the modeling process more efficient by reducing CPU, memory and storage requirements.

In summary, model evaluation in data mining is a critical step that involves the use of various tools and techniques to assess the performance and accuracy of the generated models. KNIME is a widely used tool that provides the main functionalities for data mining projects, including data integration, manipulation, visualization, model creation, validation, and reporting. Feature selection is another important aspect of model evaluation, which helps solve the problem of having too much irrelevant data or too little valuable data.

The most commonly used tools for evaluating models in data mining are Scikit-learn, Matplotlib, Seaborn, IBM Modeler, RapidMiner, KNIME and Orange. These tools offer various functionalities for data visualization, preprocessing, model building, validation and reporting, allowing analysts and data scientists to perform advanced analysis and evaluate the performance and accuracy of models.

5.   Model Evaluation and Validation

Model evaluation and validation in data mining are crucial steps to ensure the accuracy and reliability of the results. Variable selection is a common problem in data mining, and several techniques are used to address it, such as the geometric properties of estimators, the corrected or adjusted coefficient of determination, the Mallows Cp coefficient, the cross-validation method, the Akaike information criterion (AIC) and the Bayesian information criterion (BIC), and the use of software such as R

Model evaluation in data mining is also important, and involves evaluating the performance of models in absolute and relative terms, as well as comparing different models to determine which one is better.

The evaluation process includes training and testing the model, using techniques such as splitting the data into 2/3 for training and 1/3 for testing, and using different methods and problem types to compare model performance.

Model evaluation can be performed using tools such as Orange ML, which offers data visualization, preprocessing, model creation, validation and reporting functionalities.

Other tools such as Scikit-learn, Matplotlib, Seaborn, IBM Modeler, RapidMiner and KNIME are also commonly used to evaluate models in data mining.

In summary, model evaluation and validation in data mining involves several techniques and tools to ensure the accuracy and reliability of the results. Variable selection is a common problem and several techniques are used to address it. Model evaluation involves assessing the performance of models in absolute and relative terms, as well as comparing different models to determine which one is better. Tools such as Orange ML, Scikit-learn, Matplotlib, Seaborn, IBM Modeler, RapidMiner and KNIME are commonly used to evaluate models in data mining.

Model validation in data mining is performed through different methods and techniques to ensure the accuracy and reliability of the models generated.

Some of the common ways to validate models in data mining include:

Data splitting: It consists of splitting the data set into two parts, one for training the model and one for testing it. This division allows evaluating the performance of the model on data not seen during training.

Cross-validation: A technique used after creating a data mining framework and related models to determine their effectiveness. Cross-validation involves dividing the data set into multiple subsets, training the model on one part and testing it on another, repeating this process several times to obtain a more robust evaluation of the model.

Bootstrap: A resampling method that consists of creating multiple data samples from the original data set, allowing to evaluate the stability and accuracy of the model when exposed to different data sets.

Confusion matrix: It is a tool that shows the performance of a classification model, allowing to visualize the successes and errors in the prediction of the classes.

These validation methods and techniques are critical to ensure that data mining models are accurate, reliable, and generalize well to new data, which is essential for informed decision making based on data analysis.

5.1.   Evaluation Metrics

Evaluation metrics in data mining are quantitative measures used to evaluate the performance of models generated on a data set. These metrics are essential to compare different models and select those that perform better according to the project objectives. In classification problems, metrics such as Accuracy, Precision, Sensitivity, F1 score and AUC-ROC are used, while in regression problems metrics such as MAE, MSE, RMSE and R2 are used. It is essential to select the appropriate evaluation metric according to the type of problem to be solved, since each metric has a specific interpretation and may be more appropriate according to the objectives of the project.

Common evaluation metrics in data mining include:

- Accuracy: Measures the proportion of correct predictions made by the model.
- Accuracy: Indicates the proportion of correct positive predictions among all positive predictions.
- Sensitivity: Represents the proportion of positive cases that were correctly identified by the model.
- F1 score: A measure that combines accuracy and sensitivity in a single metric.
- AUC-ROC: It is the area under the receiver operating characteristic curve, which evaluates the discrimination capability of the model in classification problems.

These metrics are essential to evaluate the performance of models in data mining and are used to compare different models and select those that best fit the project objectives.

5.2. Cross Validation

Cross Validation is a technique used in data mining to evaluate the generalizability of a model. It consists of dividing the data set into multiple subsets, called "folds", where the model is trained on one part of the data and evaluated on another. This process is repeated several times, so that each subset is used for both training and evaluation, which provides a more robust estimate of model performance by avoiding overfitting to a specific data set.

On the other hand, holdout validation is a model evaluation technique in which the data set is divided into two subsets, one for training and one for validation. The main difference between the two techniques is that in cross-validation each subset is used for validation, while in holdout validation only a specific subset is used. Cross-validation is considered more robust and less susceptible to data variability, as it allows all data to be used for training and validation.

Cross Validation is essential to ensure that the model is able to generalize well to new data and is not biased by the partitioning of the data used in training and evaluation.

6.3. Overadjustment and Underadjustment

Overfitting and underfitting are two common problems in machine learning and data mining, which can affect the performance of predictive models. Overfitting occurs when a model fits the training data too closely, resulting in poor generalization to new and unseen data. Underfitting, on the other hand, occurs when a model is too simple and does not fit the training data adequately, resulting in poor performance even on the training data itself.

To address these problems, several techniques can be used. For example, cross-validation is a technique used to estimate the performance of a model by dividing the data into multiple folds and training and testing the model on each fold. This helps to ensure that the model does not overfit or underfit specific subsets of data.

Another technique is to use regularization methods, which can help avoid overfitting by adding a penalty term to the model's objective function. This penalty term encourages the model to be simpler and less prone to overfitting.

In addition, it is important to ensure that the training data are representative of the population and that there is sufficient data to train the model effectively. This can help prevent both overfitting and underfitting, as a model trained on a large and diverse data set is more likely to generalize well to new data.

In summary, overfitting and underfitting are common problems in machine learning and data mining, but there are several techniques that can be used to address them, such as cross-validation, regularization, and ensuring that the training data is representative and diverse.

6.   Application of Data Mining Models

Application of Data Mining Models refers to the process of using data mining models to extract useful patterns, relationships, and insights from large data sets. This process involves selecting appropriate data mining techniques, evaluating their performance using various metrics, and applying the best performing models to new data to generate predictions and insights.

In the context of data mining, various tools and techniques are used to evaluate and validate the performance of data mining models. For example, cross-validation is a commonly used method to estimate the accuracy of a model by dividing the data into multiple subsets and training and testing the model on each subset.

Once the models have been evaluated and validated, they can be applied to new data to generate predictions and information. This can be done using various tools and techniques, such as data mining software or programming languages like Python, which offer a wide range of libraries and tools for data mining tasks.

In summary, Data Mining Model Application involves the use of data mining models to extract useful patterns, relationships, and insights from large data sets. This process involves selecting appropriate data mining techniques, evaluating their performance using various metrics, and applying the best performing models to new data to generate predictions and insights.

7.1. Prediction and Classification

Prediction and classification are two main methods used in data mining to analyze and explore data.

Prediction is the process of identifying or predicting missing or unavailable data for a new observation based on the previous data we have.

The model used to predict the unknown value is called the predictor.

The predictor is constructed from a training set and its accuracy refers to how well it can estimate the value of new data.

Classification, on the other hand, is the process of finding a good model that describes classes of data or concepts, and the purpose of classification is to predict the class of objects whose class label is unknown.

In simple terms, we can think of classification as categorizing new incoming data based on our current or past assumptions we have had.

The model used to classify the unknown value is called a classifier.

Classifier accuracy can be referred to as the ability of the classifier to correctly predict the class label, and predictor accuracy can be referred to as how well a given predictor can estimate the unknown value.

The speed of the method depends on the computational cost of generating and using the classifier/predictor.

Robustness is the ability to make correct predictions or classifications, in the context of data mining, robustness is the ability of the classifier or predictor to make correct predictions from scalability. Scalability refers to an increase or decrease in the performance of the classifier or predictor as a function of the given.

Interpretability can refer to the ease with which we can understand the reasoning behind the predictions or classifications made.

There are mainly two main operations we need to perform on the data before applying classification or prediction methods: data cleaning and relevance analysis.

Data cleaning is the preprocessing of data, removing noise from the data, cleaning the data and correcting missing or unknown values in the data.

Relevance analysis is the analysis of data to find the relevant data according to the problem.

For example, we use correlation analysis to compare the different classes in the classification method.

After cleaning the data and analyzing it, we may need to normalize the resulting data, because normalized data provides more accuracy in predicting an unknown value.

Normalization can be achieved by scaling all the values of the data set from 0 to 1 in the range

Classification and prediction are related but different concepts in data mining. Classification involves predicting the class label of a new observation based on training data, while prediction involves estimating the value of a continuous variable.

Both methods are important in data mining and are used to extract patterns, relationships and useful knowledge from large data sets.

Classification and prediction are two common techniques used in data mining to analyze and extract useful information from large data sets. Classification is the process of categorizing data into different classes according to certain characteristics, while prediction is the process of predicting future trends or events based on historical data.

In the context of data mining, classification is used to identify patterns and relationships in data, which can be used to make predictions about future events or behavior.

Classification models are trained on labeled data, which means that the data have already been categorized into different classes.

The model learns to recognize patterns and relationships between data features and corresponding class labels, and can then be used to predict the class label of new unlabeled data.

Forecasting, on the other hand, is the process of using historical data to make predictions about future events or trends.

Predictive models are trained on historical data and use statistical or machine learning algorithms to identify patterns and relationships between data characteristics and the target variable.

Once the model has been trained, it can be used to make predictions about new and unseen data based on the patterns and relationships it has learned from historical data.

In summary, classification and prediction are two important techniques used in data mining to analyze and extract useful information from large data sets. Classification is used to categorize data into different classes according to certain characteristics, while prediction is used to predict future trends or events based on historical data.

Both techniques are used to identify patterns and relationships in the data, which can be used to make informed decisions and predictions about future events or behavior.

7.2. Grouping and segmentation

Clustering and segmentation are two related but distinct concepts in data mining, which involve organizing data into groups or categories based on certain characteristics or attributes.

Clustering, also known as clustering, is a technique used to group similar data points based on their attributes or characteristics. The goal of clustering is to identify patterns or structures in the data that are not immediately obvious and to group similar data points in a way that makes sense. Clustering can be used for a variety of purposes, such as identifying customer segments, detecting fraud, or identifying patterns in medical data.

Segmentation, on the other hand, is the process of dividing a population or data set into smaller groups based on certain characteristics or attributes. The goal of segmentation is to create homogeneous groups that are similar in some respect, such as demographics, behavior or preferences. Segmentation is often used in marketing and advertising to target specific groups of customers or to understand customer behavior.

In summary, clustering and segmentation are techniques used to organize data into groups or categories, but they differ in their objectives and methods. Clustering focuses on identifying patterns or structures in the data, while segmentation focuses on dividing a population or set of data into homogeneous groups based on certain characteristics or attributes.

7.3. Association of Rules

The term "Association Rules" refers to Association Rules in the context of data mining and machine learning. Association rules are used to discover common patterns or relationships within a specific data set. These rules are based on the concept of identifying associations between different elements or variables in the data. By analyzing these associations, valuable insights can be gained, such as understanding which items are frequently purchased together in a supermarket or identifying patterns in customer behavior.

Association rules are widely used in a variety of fields, including shopping cart analysis, web mining, intrusion detection and bioinformatics. They help uncover hidden patterns and relationships that can be leveraged for decision-making processes, such as targeted marketing strategies or personalized recommendations.

In summary, "Rule Association" plays a crucial role in data mining by revealing interesting relationships and patterns within data sets, which can lead to valuable insights and informed decision making.

7.   Ethical and Legal Considerations

Ethical and legal considerations in data mining are critical to ensure privacy, consent, transparency and data protection.

Anonymization is a technique used to protect the privacy of individuals, but it is not foolproof and can make it difficult to detect bias or other problems in data mining algorithms. Data mining needs a code of ethics, as day-to-day evidence indicates that not all information from data mining presupposes that the individual gives them the information they generate with credit card, phone usage, etc. The user can indicate otherwise, but to do so they must write a letter and mail it to the company's headquarters, which involves culture, time and expense. The code of ethics is necessary to ensure that data mining is done ethically and responsibly, and to unlock the full potential of data mining while protecting the rights of individuals. Data mining has become an essential tool for BDCs to identify trends, investment opportunities, improve marketing strategies and make better informed decisions about investments, marketing and other aspects of the business.

The main ethical concerns in data mining include privacy, consent, transparency, and accountability. These concerns arise from the potential for data mining to be used to collect and analyze personal information without the individual's knowledge or consent, which can lead to privacy violations, discrimination, and other negative impacts. To address these concerns, ethical guidelines and frameworks, such as the ACM Code of Ethics, GDPR and the Asilomar AI Principles, should be followed to ensure that data mining aligns with the values and interests of stakeholders. Data mining should also be subject to deliberation, consultation and ethical evaluation, and consider the potential benefits and harms to society and the environment. In addition, measures must be taken to ensure data quality, privacy, security, scalability and ethical considerations, such as obtaining informed consent, using encryption, firewalls and backups, monitoring and auditing data mining activities, and reporting and responding to any security incidents or breaches. Ethical considerations are crucial in genetic data mining, where sensitive genetic information is involved, and in business decision making, where data mining can provide valuable information but must be approached ethically and responsibly to avoid potential risks and negative impacts.

9.1. Data Privacy

Data privacy in data mining refers to the ability of individuals to control the collection and use that is made of their data. Data mining is an analytical process that identifies hidden patterns and systematic relationships within data, with the ultimate goal of prediction and business application.

Privacy, consent and ownership are related concepts when it comes to user data. Privacy is defined as the state of being free from public attention, and the boundary between private and public is considered violated when the ownership of customers' personal data is breached and publicly exposed.

Information technology (IT) comes in many forms, such as laptops, smartphones, the Internet, cloud gaming, cell phone applications, and the daily lives of individuals are increasingly dependent on technology, which continues to record, communicate, synthesize and organize any data that is useful about them and collect data for their use

Data privacy is a critical issue for businesses and individuals alike, as the digital age brings with it invaluable benefits but also significant concerns about the collection and storage of personal and confidential information.

Data privacy refers to safeguarding personal and confidential data against unauthorized access, use and disclosure, while data protection includes data privacy and data security.

Data security is vital to prevent data leaks and cyber attacks, while data privacy is essential to maintain confidentiality and protect users' privacy rights.

Accountability and Transparency

Data mining is a process of discovering patterns and insights from large amounts of data. It is important to ensure that data mining is conducted responsibly and transparently to protect the rights of individuals and maintain trust. The following are some key considerations for responsible and transparent data mining:

Ethics: data mining should be conducted in accordance with ethical guidelines and frameworks, such as the ACM Code of Ethics, the GDPR or the Asilomar AI Principles, to ensure that it aligns with the values and interests of stakeholders.

Consideration of benefits and harms: data mining should consider potential benefits and harms to society and the environment, and engage in ethical deliberations, consultations and evaluations.

Data quality: Data mining must ensure data quality, including accuracy, completeness and relevance, to ensure reliable and meaningful results.

Privacy: Data mining must protect the privacy of individuals by obtaining informed consent, using encryption, firewalls or backups, and monitoring and auditing data mining activities.

Security: Data mining must ensure data security by preventing or mitigating the risks of data breaches or losses, and by reporting and responding to any security incidents or breaches.

Transparency: data mining must be transparent in its methods, objectives and results, and provide clear and understandable explanations to stakeholders.

Accountability: Data mining should be accountable for its actions and decisions, and provide mechanisms for remediation and correction in case of errors or violations.

Following these considerations, data mining can be carried out in a responsible and transparent manner, ensuring the protection of individual rights and maintaining trust.

9.3. Regulatory Compliance

Regulatory compliance in data mining is crucial to ensure the protection of privacy and the rights of individuals. Regulations, such as the General Data Protection Regulation (GDPR) in the European Union, establish guidelines for the ethical and lawful use of personal data. It is critical that organizations conducting data mining comply with these regulations to avoid potential penalties and protect the confidentiality of the information collected. In addition, compliance with regulations such as GDPR involves obtaining appropriate consent from individuals for the processing of their data, ensuring information security, and respecting the privacy rights of individuals. In short, regulatory compliance in data mining is essential to ensure transparency, accountability, and respect for the privacy of users' data.

The General Data Protection Regulation (GDPR) is a regulation that governs data protection and privacy in the European Union (EU) and the European Economic Area (EEA). It is a comprehensive regulation that establishes a single set of rules for the protection of personal data in all EU member states. The GDPR applies to all companies that process personal data of EU residents, regardless of where the company is located.

The GDPR establishes specific rights for individuals with respect to their personal data, including the right to access, rectify, delete, object to processing and data portability. It also imposes obligations on data controllers and processors, including the obligation to obtain consent, implement appropriate technical and organizational measures to ensure the security of personal data, and notify data breaches to supervisory authorities and affected individuals.

The GDPR provides for significant penalties for non-compliance, including fines of up to 4% of global annual revenue or €20 million (whichever is greater). It also establishes a new regulatory framework for data protection, including the creation of a European Data Protection Board (EDPB) to oversee the implementation of the GDPR and ensure consistency across EU member states.

The GDPR is a complex regulation that requires careful consideration and planning to ensure compliance. It is important that companies understand the requirements of the GDPR and take appropriate steps to ensure compliance, including implementing appropriate technical and organizational measures to protect personal data, obtaining consent where necessary, and providing individuals with the rights and remedies required by the GDPR.

Data mining is a strategic tool that raises the levels of competence in the business world by enabling the rapid identification and analysis of relevant information for effective decision making.

The ability to store data has grown exponentially, but it is critical to have techniques that can process and understand both structured and unstructured data to support decision making in a variety of domains.

Data mining provides significant advantages, such as ease of use and applicability of appropriate knowledge, but it also requires additional effort in establishing performance evaluation measures.

By converting data into evaluated information and knowledge for action, data mining provides the necessary support for informed decision making that guides companies towards achieving their goals and objectives.

These findings highlight the importance and positive impact that data mining can have on organizations by providing valuable information for strategic decision making and improving business competitiveness.

References

Ackoff, Russell L. (1989). "From data to wisdom." Journal of applied systems analysis, no. 16, p. 3-9.

Agrawal, Rakesh; Imielinski, Tomasz; Swami, Arun (1993). "Mining association rules between sets of items in large databases". Proceedings of the 1993 ACM SIGMOD Conference. <http://rakesh.agrawal-family.com/papers/sigmod93assoc.pdf>. [Accessed: 1-05-2006].

Agrawal, Rakesh; Srinkant, Ramakrishnan (2000). "Privacy-preserving data mining". Proceedings of the 2000 ACM SIGMOD conference on management of data. p. 439-450. <http://doi.acm.org/10.1145/342009.335438> . [Accessed: 1-05-2006].

American Library Association. The USA patriot act in the library. <http://www.ala.org/ala/oif/ifissues/usapatriotactlibrary.htm>. [Accessed: 30-04-2006].

Banerjee, K. (1998). "Is data mining right for your library?" Computers in libraries, vol. 18, no. 10, pp. 28-31.

Bellinger, Gene; Castro, Durval; Mills, Anthony (1994). Data, information, knowledge, and wisdom. <http://www.systems-thinking.org/dikw/dikw.htm>.[Accessed: 1-05-2006].

Bereijo Martínez, Antonio (1998). "Characterization of the concept of 'quality' in descriptive cataloging: factors that concern the design of objectives." Millares Carlo Bulletin, No. 17, p. 319-355. <http://dialnet.unirioja.es/servlet/fichero_articulo?articulo=1700760&orden=37277>. [Consultation: 12/04/2006].

Bollen, Johan; Luce, Rick; Vemulapalli, Soma Sekhara; Weining, Xu (2003). "Usage analysis for the identification of research trends in digital libraries". D-lib magazine, May, vol. 9, no. 5, <http://www.dlib.org/dlib/may03/bollen/05bollen.html. [Accessed 31-03-2006].

Borgman, Christine L. (1986). "Why are online catalogs hard to use? Lessons learned from information-retrieval studies" Journal of the American society for information science, vol. 37, no. 6, p. 387-400. <http://www3.interscience.wiley.com/cgi-bin/abstract/57783/>. [Accessed 7-05-2006].

Brin, Sergey; Motwani, Rajeev; Ullman, Jeffrey D.; Tsur, Shalom (1997). "Dynamic itemset counting and implication rules for market basket data". Proceedings of the 1997 ACM SIGMOD conference. p. 255-264 <http://doi.acm.org/10.1145/253260.253325>. [Accessed: 1-05-2006].

Casey, Michael (2005). "Working towards a definition of Library 2.0". Library Crunch: bringing you a library 2.0 perspective, October 21, 2005. <http://www.librarycrunch.com/2005/10/working_towards_a_definition_o.htm>. [Accessed 16-05-2006].

Chi-Wing Wong, Raymond; Wai-Chee Fu, Ada; Wang, Ke (2005). "Data mining for inventory item selection with cross-selling considerations". Data mining and knowledge discovery, July 2005, vol. 11, no. 1, p. 81-112.

Cleveland, Harland (1982). "Information as resource". The futurist, December, p. 34-39.

Clifton, Chris; Doan, Anhai; Elmagarmid, Ahmed; Kantarcioglu, Murat; Schadow, Gunther; Suciu, Dan; Vaidya, Jaideep (2004). "Privacy preserving, data integration and sharing". Data mining and knowledge discovery archive. Proceedings of the 9th ACM SIGMOD workshop on research issues in data mining and knowledge discovery. p. 19-26. <http://doi.acm.org/10.1145/1008694.1008698>. [Consulta: 21-04-2006].

Cox, Kenneth C.; Eick, Stephen G.; Wills, Graham J.; Brachman, Ronald J. (1997). "Brief application description; visual data mining: recognizing telephone calling fraud". Data mining and knowledge discovery, June, vol. 1, no. 2, p. 225-231.

Crawford, Walt (2006). "Library 2.0 and 'Library 2.0'." Cites & insights, vol. 6, no. 2, p. 1-32. <http://cites.boisestate.edu/civ6i2.pdf> [Accessed 16-05-2006].

Cullen, Kelvin (2005). "Delving into data". Library journal August, vol. 130, no. 13, p. 30-32. <http://www.libraryjournal.com/article/CA633325.html>. [Accessed: 26-04-2006].

Domingo-Ferrer, Josep; Torra, Vicenç (2005). "Privacy in data mining". Data mining and knowledge discovery, September, vol. 11, no. 2, p. 117-119.

Domínguez Sanjurjo, Mª Ramona (1996). New forms of organization and services in the public library. Gijón: Trea

Spain. "Ley orgánica 15/1999, de 13 de diciembre, de protección de datos de carácter personal". oletín Oficial del Estado, 14 de diciembre de 1999, núm. 298, p. 43088-43099.

Fawcett, Tom; Provost, Foster (1997). "Adaptive fraud detection". Data mining and knowledge discovery, September, vol. 1, no. 3, p. 291-316.

Fayyad, Usama M.; Piatetsky-Shapiro, Gregory; Smyth, Padhraic (1996). "From data mining to knowledge discovery: an overview". In: Fayyad, Usama M.; Piatetsky-Shapiro, Gregory; Smyth, Padhraic (ed.). Advances in knowledge discovery and data mining. California: AAAI Press, The MIT Press, p. 1-36.

Fayyad, Usama; Simoudis, Evangelos (1995). Knowledge discovery and data mining. <http://www-aig.jpl.nasa.gov/public/kdd95/tutorials/IJCAI95-tutorial.html>   . [Accessed: 1-05-2006].

Fayyad, Usama; Uthurusamy, Ramasamy (1996). "Data mining and knowledge discovery in databases". Communications of the ACM, November, vol. 39, no. 11, p. 24-26. <http://doi.acm.org/10.1145/240455.240463> . [Accessed: 1-05-2006].

International Federation of Library Associations and Institutions; United Nations Educational, Scientific and Cultural Organization (2001). IFLA/UNESCO guidelines for the development of public library service. 94 p. <http://www.ifla.org/VII/s8/news/pg01-s.pdf>. [Accessed 4-04-2006].

Fernández Molina, Juan Carlos; Moya Anegón, Félix de (1998). Online public access catalogs: the future of bibliographic information retrieval. Málaga: Asociación Andaluza de Bibliotecarios, 197 p.

Geyer-Schulz, Andreas; Neumann, Andreas; Thede, Anke (2003). "An architecture for behavior-based library recommender systems". Information technology and libraries, 2003, vol. 22, no. 4, p. 165-174. <http://www.ala.org/ala/lita/litapublications/ital/2204geyer.htm . [Accessed 23-08-2006]

Gómez-Pantoja Fernández-Salguero, Aurora; Pérez Pulido, Margarita (1998). "El concepto de privacidad en servicios bibliotecarios actuales". FESABID 98. VI Jornadas Españolas de Documentación: los sistemas de información al servicio de la sociedad. <http://fesabid98.florida-uni.es/Comunicaciones/a_gomez.htm>. [Consultation: 15-06-2006].

Guenther, Kim (2000). "Applying data mining principles to a library data collection." Computers in libraries, vol. 20, no. 4, p. 60-63.

Hand, David; Mannila, Heikki; Smyth, Padric (2001). Principles of data mining. Cambridge: Massachusetts Institute of Technology.

Hernández, Hilario (dir.) (2003). Las colecciones de las bibliotecas públicas en España: informe de situación. Salamanca: Fundación Germán Sánchez Ruipérez.

Hernández Orallo, José; Ramírez Quintana, Mª José; Ferri Ramírez, Cèsar (2004). Introducción a la minería de datos. Madrid: Pearson - Prentice Hall.

Houghton, Sarah (2005). "Library 2.0 Discussion: Michael Squared". LibraryInBlack.net: resources and discussions for the 'tech-librarians-by-default' among us... December 19. <http://librarianinblack.typepad.com/librarianinblack/2005/12/library_20_disc.html>. [Accessed: 16-05-2006].

Kao, S.-C.; Chang, H.-C.; Lin, C.-H. (2003). "Decision support for the academic library acquisition budget allocation via circulation database mining". Information processing and management, no. 39, p. 133-147. Knowledge discovery and data mining conference (KDD-95). <http://www-aig.jpl.nasa.gov/public/kdd95/>. [Accessed: 1-05-2006].

Kohavi, Ron (2001). "Mining e-commerce data: the good, the bad, and the ugly". Conference on Knowledge Discovery in Data Archive: proceedings of the seventh ACM SIGKDD International Conference on Knowledge Discovery and Data Mining. p. 8-13. <http://doi.acm.org/10.1145/502512.502518>. [Consulta: 1-05-2006].